RYSZARD KRYNICKI, one of Poland's most important contemporary poets, was born in a labor camp in Sankt Valentin (Lower Austria) in 1943. Since the 1960s, when he became known as one of the poets of the New Wave, Krynicki has been associated with the democratic opposition in Poland. As a result, he was subjected to censorship and then banned completely from official publication between 1976 and 1980, although he continued to publish with unofficial presses and, in the case of *Our Life Grows* (1978), with the Paris émigré press Kultura. After working for years as an editor in underground publishing and running a private art gallery with his wife, Krystyna, in their Poznań apartment, he founded the influential publishing house a5 in 1988; from the start, the press focused on contemporary Polish poetry, including the works of Wisława Szymborska, Adam Zagajewski, and many younger poets. Krynicki is also renowned as a translator of German-language poets, including Nelly Sachs and Paul Celan. A recipient of many prestigious literary awards, he was most recently awarded the Zbigniew Herbert International Poetry Prize in 2015. He lives in Kraków.

ALISSA VALLES is the author of the poetry books *Orphan Fire* (2008) and *Anastylosis* (2014) and the editor and cotranslator of Zbigniew Herbert's *Collected Poems* and *Collected Prose*.

ADAM MICHNIK is a Polish newspaper editor, writer, and historian. He was jailed by the 〔   〕ᵗ government in 1968 and twice more in the 19〔   〕 about postwar Eastern Europe〔   〕 a totalitarian regime, and mor〔   〕

D0828008

Ryszard Krynicki

Our Life Grows
(Uncensored)

TRANSLATED FROM THE POLISH AND
WITH AN INTRODUCTION BY
ALISSA VALLES
AFTERWORD BY ADAM MICHNIK

NYRB/POETS

 NEW YORK REVIEW BOOKS   *New York*

THIS IS A NEW YORK REVIEW BOOK
PUBLISHED BY THE NEW YORK REVIEW OF BOOKS
435 Hudson Street, New York, NY 10014
www.nyrb.com

This book has been published with the support
of the ©POLAND Translation program.

Library of Congress Cataloging-in-Publication data
Names: Krynicki, Ryszard, 1943– author. | Valles, Alissa, translator. |
  Michnik, Adam, writer of afterword.
Title: Our life grows / by Ryszard Krynicki ; translated by Alissa Valles ;
  afterword by Adam Michnik.
Other titles: Nasze życie rośnie. English
Description: New York : New York Review Books, [2017] | Series: New York
  Review Books Poets |
Identifiers: LCCN 2017038180 (print) | LCCN 2017038627 (ebook) | ISBN
  9781681371610 (epub) | ISBN 9781681371603 (paperback)
Subjects: | BISAC: POETRY / Continental European.
Classification: LCC PG7170.R9 (ebook) | LCC PG7170.R9 N313 2017 (print)
  | DDC 891.8/517—dc23
LC record available at https://lccn.loc.gov/2017038180

ISBN 978-1-68137-160-3
Available as an electronic book; ISBN 978-1-68137-161-0

Cover and book design by Emily Singer

Printed in the United States of America on acid-free paper.
10 9 8 7 6 5 4 3 2 1

Contents

INTRODUCTION

> *De quoi faut-il donc nourrir la poésie pour lui garder ce qu'elle a d'indomptable?** *
> —PAUL CELAN TO GISÈLE CELAN-LESTRANGE

RYSZARD KRYNICKI was born in the Nazi labor camp Windberg in Sankt Valentin, not far from Vienna, in the dark year of 1943. His parents had been deported there from Kozova in what was eastern Poland and is now Ukraine; in May 1945, his father, Stanisław, was forced to join the Red Army and it was not until 1947 that he could return to his family, now resettled in western Poland. By the time Krynicki started school, Stalinists had consolidated their hold on the Polish state. An avid reader from early on, he has said that as a teenager, thanks to his encounters with books—especially those of Edgar Allan Poe, Franz Kafka, and Bruno Schulz—he lived in a "half-mythical world, though those were the years of Stalinism." In 1961 he entered Poznań University, where he studied Polish literature and was active as an editor of and contributor to student publications; he left the university before completing a master's thesis on

---

*On what should one feed poetry in order to preserve what is untameable in it?

vii

the avant-garde poet Julian Przyboś. It was in Poznań in the mid-sixties that he formed a vital friendship with his fellow poet Stanisław Barańczak.

As young poets, Krynicki and Barańczak were soon recognized as leading representatives of what came to be called the Nowa Fala, or New Wave, in Polish poetry. This generation of poets, which also included Julian Kornhauser, Ewa Lipska, Adam Zagajewski, and Rafał Wojaczek—who died very young by his own hand—found themselves, as Krynicki said in a later interview, "unable to be silent any longer" in the face of state-imposed falsehoods. Despite Stalin's death and Khrushchev's thaw, Poland in 1968 was a society poisoned and paralyzed by political repression, economic corruption, censorship of the press and the arts, and state-sponsored campaigns against Jews and intellectuals. The New Wave poets were very different from one another, but they all felt a need to confront the lies, cruelties, and injustices of the Communist regime directly, and some of them felt that the poetry of the previous generation had so far failed to do so. At a poetry festival in 1972, Krynicki publicly criticized Zbigniew Herbert on this count—as too oblique, too allegorical in his poetic responses to the political present. Before long, Herbert became a close friend and mentor, and he later dedicated to the younger poet one of his greatest poems, "To Ryszard Krynicki—A Letter," which addresses the question of how much of his gift a poet owes to his or her times, how much to the timeless riddles of existence.

Krynicki's first two collections, *Akt Urodzenia* (Birth Certificate, 1969) and *Organizm Zbiórowy* (Collective Organism, 1975), appeared in editions mangled by the censor. One early poem, "Our Special Correspondent," included in this book, has a particularly colorful history. Even under the coy title "The Discovery of America," it was cut from the first collection; it was then published in the journal *Odra* in 1971, where it was the principal reason the renowned poet Tymoteusz Karpowicz lost his position as editor. Included in the manuscript of *Collective Organism*, scheduled to appear with the state publisher Czytelnik in the brief period of relaxed censorship that lasted from 1971 to 1973, the poem was one of fifteen the poet was "requested" to eliminate in a letter he received from the publisher in the summer of 1972. Krynicki refused, and instead printed "Our Special Correspondent" in a small samizdat chapbook edition titled *Wszystko jest możliwe* (Everything's Possible) in 1973.

From this period on Krynicki suffered repeated harassment by the Polish security police. In an interview he recalled: "We as a family were subjected to more than twenty house searches, and it even happened that our daughter was searched on the way to school, to check that she wasn't carrying anything for us. Her school class went on a trip to Budapest but Natalia had to stay at home. She had no passport." When attempting to cross the border into Austria in 1973 to take up a yearlong fellowship in Vienna for which Herbert had nominated him, Krynicki was detained and accused of smuggling narcotics. Another protracted censorship struggle followed with the Kraków publisher Wydawnictwo Literackie, where *Collective Organism* finally appeared, with cuts, in 1975. That same year, after Krynicki put his signature to a letter protesting changes in the constitution, part of this edition was destroyed.

In 1976 Krynicki became the subject of a complete publication ban, which meant not only that he could not publish anything officially but that his name could not be mentioned in print. However, Krynicki's work as a poet and editor under the official radar continued undiminished throughout the Communist years; in addition to collaborating with a number of literary periodicals, he co-edited the underground newspaper *Obserwator Wielkopolski* for more than seven years following the introduction of martial law in 1981. He and his wife, Krystyna, also organized clandestine art exhibits in their Poznań apartment, a space they called Galeria bez miejsca, or Gallery Without a Place. Visual art always had an important place in Krynicki's creative and personal life, and he collaborated with artist friends such as Zbylut Grzywacz, Leszek Sobocki, and Henryk Waniek on publications combining word and image. He was particularly influenced by the spiritual investigations and Zen practice of an artists' group called Oneiron, which was co-founded by Waniek; Waniek's surrealist drawings accompanying Krynicki's poems in several publications convey a sense of mystery in elemental landscapes and things—stone, glass, water, night skies—close to Krynicki's own visionary geography.

The year in Vienna—where he was finally permitted to travel in 1977 and 1978—provided Krynicki with an opportunity to study German and to read intensively a number of poets who became vital interlocutors. His translations of Paul Celan and Nelly Sachs had a profound impact on his own poems (first appearing alongside them in the samizdat booklet *Wiersze, glossy*—Poems, Voices—in 1985). In 1998 he edited a bilingual selection of his own Celan translations and those of many others, and in the following years he published large selections of his own translations of Sachs and Celan. There were also occasional translations of poems by contemporaries like Reiner Kunze and Sarah Kirsch and earlier poets like Joseph von Eichendorff, Wilhelm Klemm, and Bertolt Brecht.

In 1977 Krynicki won the prestigious Kościelskich Prize, which after considerable delay he was able to collect in Geneva, and the following year the collection *Our Life Grows* appeared with the émigré press Kultura at the Literary Institute in Paris, in the series Bez cenzury (Uncensored), a series that also included essays by Adam Michnik, by then one of the most prominent leaders of the democratic opposition. *Kultura*—the journal and the institute—had become the political and moral headquarters of free Polish cultural life after World War II. Its legendary director Jerzy Giedroyc and his colleagues published Józef Czapski, Witold Gombrowicz, Gustaw Herling-Grudziński, Zbigniew Herbert, Czesław Miłosz, and Aleksander Wat, as well as Polish-language editions of writers like Albert Camus and Raymond Aron. *Our Life Grows* marked Krynicki's appearance on the wider stage of European literature.

Our Life Grows captures a poet at a crucial point in his development, a time where early inspirations—especially the Polish avant-garde poet Tadeusz Peiper and the Baroque poet Mikołaj Sęp Szarzyński—combine with the growing influence of Herbert and the German poets.

Barańczak suggested that Krynicki traveled a path "from excess to ascesis"; it strikes me that many of his most powerful poems are ones in which these contrary impulses are contained and held in dynamic opposition. "The Tongue, That Untamed Flesh" and "You Are," for example, have an energy that springs from a cascading stream of image and metaphor meeting a stringent inward filter. From the performative rage and mockery of the early political poems, the movement is toward a purification of language from within, through Celanian silence and Herbertian skepticism (from Greek "σκέπτομαι" *skeptomai*, to search). *Our Life Grows* embodies this crystallization, which is why it is important that it be read in its entirety.

The section of earlier work that concludes the collection includes those poems cut from *Collective Organism*, or which had been published only in a truncated or otherwise distorted form. In one of these, the poet's sea change is expressed lucidly. "Not a Poem but a Confession," like many of Krynicki's writings, exists in several versions. The early version, included here, speaks of a third person who "stopped amusing us" with a "play of appearances." By 1989, this became a first-person confession and a more precise self-diagnosis: "I caused dismay when I stopped using / wordplay to amuse, the helpless mimicry / of slaves" (translated by Clare Cavanagh). These different, evolving versions of poems are central to Krynicki's mature view of the poem as an open form. In a real sense for him, poems are never finished, they remain perpetually open to change, correction, rereading, and renewal.

From its second poem on Franz Kafka, and Max Brod's

decision to preserve rather than destroy his writings, *Our Life Grows* makes explicit Krynicki's skepticism about the place of literature in human culture (a list of his favorite books always includes *Don Quixote* and *Madame Bovary*). Not only German poets but also periods of immersion in non-Western poetry and thought encouraged a tendency toward an ever greater uncertainty about the human capacity to know, let alone speak, truth. The main body of this collection ends with the barest clutch of certainties, the most confident of which is that the speaker "doesn't know." Perhaps related to this is Krynicki's marked discomfort with the notion of "being a poet": "I prefer to avoid that word, talking about myself." He identifies himself with greater ease as an editor, a translator, a publisher, a reader, a librarian—he did over the years hold positions in three scholarly libraries—or a custodian, not simply of books but of voices.

Our Life Grows was published in underground versions in Poland in 1980 and 1981, and followed by the chapbook *Niewiele wiecej: wiersze z notatnika 1978/79* (Not Much More: Poems from a Notebook 1978/79). Many of these notebook poems are aphorisms with a direct connection to the period of political struggle that culminated in martial law, and the subsequent drawn-out showdown with the Communist state, during which Krynicki was a familiar face at democratic protests.

"You're free," says the guard
and the iron gate closes

from the other side this time

By the time the Communist era came to an end in 1989, Krynicki was in his mid-forties. It is not surprising that the nature of freedom has always been one of his central preoccupations as a poet, and one that he has often approached through the many guises of unfreedom—lies, censorship, captivity, slavery, and violence. But from the first his poems tended to be at once political and metaphysical, their historical irony and spiritual questioning infused with powerful eroticism. Krynicki is one of the great and rare love poets of postwar Europe; like John Donne's, his erotic poems fuse physical concreteness with oneiric fantasy and often political suggestion: "Her weary body / refuses to obey, / refuses mutely." One of the occasions of comedy in his poems is the collision of worlds usually kept separate and described in different languages. In the prologue poem, "I Believe," the freedom to pursue a lover, take a trip, and think telepathic thoughts are not standard components of any orthodox credo. The poem also breaks decorum roundly by pointing to the censor as a co-editor, crossing out "words that could come back to haunt me." It is worth mentioning in this context that Krynicki was repeatedly pressured to remove the name of Osip Mandelstam from this poem, but refused.

When in 1989 Krynicki's selected poems and translations *Niepodlegli nicości* (Independent of Nothingness) appeared, it was still with the mark of the censor. In its negotiations with the Communist government, Solidarity had managed to win a concession: the censor's intrusions now had to be clearly indicated in the published text, so that where a poem was cut, a note at the bottom of the page cited

the relevant article of the penal code. This pregnant paren-
thesis appears in the book six times. In the same period,
Krynicki and his wife set up their own publishing house,
Wydawnictwo a5, which became one of the most distin-
guished Polish publishers, particularly for poetry: beginning
with Barańczak, they soon became the publishers of exqui-
sitely designed and printed volumes of the work of Zbig-
niew Herbert and Wisława Szymborska, Julia Hartwig and
Adam Zagajewski, and a whole raft of younger poets, in-
cluding Tomasz Różycki, Marcin Świetlicki, and Marcin
Sendecki.

In 1998 the Krynickis moved themselves and their pub-
lishing enterprise to Kraków, where they continue to live.
After a period of relative reticence during which he published
—apart from numerous foreign translations of his work—
only the selection of poems and translations *Magnetyczny
Punkt* (Magnetic Point, 1996), Krynicki reemerged in 2004
with the new poetry collection *Kamień, szroń* (Stone, Hoar-
frost), which won him a nomination for Poland's major lit-
erary prize, the Nike Award. In the years that followed,
large selections of his poems appeared, and there have been
a number of reprints of early collections or sequences, in-
cluding a 1971 chapbook of collage text entitled *G*, which
was reissued in 2014 by MOCAK, the Museum of Contem-
porary Art in Kraków.

The sequence *G*, subtitled a "funerary panegyric" and
made up of words and phrases cut from newspapers, is framed
by two cutout images: The first, on the front cover, is of an
open mouth, seemingly in mid-speech or song, impossible
to identify as male or female. The second is a photograph of

two men in loincloths, one of them with his hand covering the eyes of a third figure, a naked boy; the other man is apparently preparing to circumcise the boy with an instrument he holds in his right hand. Krynicki's poetry as a whole takes place between that open mouth with its untamed tongue and the blind force acting on the boy, dictating his place in the hierarchy of generations and genders, and of man and God, whose law or will seems to be implied in the ritualistic (eerily staged) quality of the scene.

The question of what keeps poetry untamed is in the largest sense one about its relation to time: Celan, quoted at the beginning of this introduction, reflecting in a letter on a friend's writing, is asking in the first instance what makes poetry endure, what allows it not to become dated but to remain independent of Shakespeare's "Devouring Time" that blunts "the lion's paws." Reading Krynicki, one finds that the philosophical question enfolds the political one. In the reactionary climate of contemporary Poland, his poems have the same political claws that they had when first written; but if you take them as the most serious kind of response to Celan's question, they seem to answer: We tried scorn, satire, and the spirit of contention, and what we have ended up with is: love. By which I think they mean the love, at once erotic and spiritual, of the Song of Solomon (8:6), a love that embraces the living and the dead; love that is "as strong as death."

—*Alissa Valles*

Our Life Grows

For Krystynka and Natalia

An unknown spy will send him a challenge
A perjured court will do battle with him
— ADAM MICKIEWICZ
"Do Matki Polki" (To a Polish Mother)

I rebelled
but I think this bloody knot
should be the very last one
a man freeing himself
should tear loose
— ZBIGNIEW HERBERT
"Reflections on the Problem of the Nation"

You survived not so that you might live
you have little time you must give testimony
— ZBIGNIEW HERBERT
"The Envoy of Mr. Cogito"

and in that weeping
there is always
so much life
— STANISŁAW BARAŃCZAK
"The Day After Tomorrow"

This, Nothing
Or, Other Poems for Internal Use

If it is true that the same suffering is harder to endure for noble reasons than for base ones (people who have stood motionless in a queue from one o'clock at night to eight in the morning to obtain an egg would have had great difficulty doing the same to save a human life), it may be that virtue of a base kind is more resistant to adversity, temptation and misfortune than virtue of a noble kind.

◆ ◆ ◆

We know from experience that the truth is always universal and reality is always particular, and yet they are inseparable and even form a whole. We can find no way out of this problem.

—SIMONE WEIL

I Believe

for Stanisław and Anna Barańczak

The truth is: at times I believe
in the existence of the other world, I believe in ghosts,
in vampires sucking your brain and blood,
perhaps in the end I fear even more than believe
(which comes to the same thing in our time: to fear—to
    believe).
At those times I try not to sit with my back to the door,
a door has a life of its own, and what's more,
I've become superstitious, I don't talk about my dreams
or hopes aloud anymore, so I don't scare them off, I avoid
uttering words that could come back to haunt me,
I cross them out of old poems (and for that matter
not only I), but I won't hide the fact
that I sometimes forget these measures of security,
drink vodka, love a woman, go on a trip, think
telepathic thoughts, turn my back
to the door—which has its own life
and sooner or later will open,
and sooner or later I'll feel the touch
of that icy hand, which may only give me a sign
or may without warning tighten around my heart,
the truth is: I don't believe this is the hand
of Osip Mandelstam or Georg Trakl,
or of any other poet who, independently of the human
or inhuman death he met,

still speaks to us with his living words.

Did Max Brod, Called "Dearest"

Did Max Brod, called "Dearest Max,"
have the right not to fulfill the last request
of a dying friend
already reconciled to love and death;
did he have the right,
choosing between literature
and loyalty,
to betray his friend
with her,

with literature, who can be a killer
devoid of all pity
even when she spares her victims,

even if she spares her victims
in order to subject them to still crueler trials
and torments?

Why did Franz Kafka, when
he was already reconciled to love and death
and no longer needed to put to the test
either his friends or his defenseless characters,
pass sentence on his own books?

Did he take pity
and, at the last, wish to shield us from them?
Had he come to think that any vision of evil
will embody itself in a real evil
outstripping our worst fears and premonitions?

Did he have another reason
we'll never understand, we
posthumous children of the cruelest of wars,
in which Franz Kafka, a star on his forehead,
might have died a million times in the street,
in ghettos and camps,
and his books have been burned on pyres
and smoldered in the rubble of houses?

Maybe to us,
posthumous children of the cruelest of wars
living in a time of cruel peace,
it only seems that way—
you can't imagine
an even greater cruelty

because lies and violence
once they exist
will not cease until they wipe from the face of the Earth
the slightest trace of disobedience?

Buddha, Christ

Buddha, Christ,

in vain you hide
in so many incarnations

Caute

*He left a few dozen books, a couple of copperplate
engravings, a green overcoat, a quilt, seven shirts
and a few other items.*
—LESZEK KOŁAKOWSKI

Cautiously you unclench your hand, it's
blind and dumb. Shameless, stripped naked. Fingerprinted,
entered in the index. Spinoza's friends no longer
exist, nor do those who repudiated him,
nor those who feasted on his warm body,
nor the worms that fed on his flesh,
nor his enemies,
nor the inquisitors of his time,
nor the clouds that crossed the borders of his time,
nor are the reasons for his death now timely;
his overcoat, quilt and shirts
no longer clothe anyone, there are new books in new
   bookstores,
exiles in exile, fingerprints
in files, reinforcements on borders, files in cabinets,
customs officers on target, residents in residences, sales
   staff in stores,
typescripts in drawers, simpers on lips, blood
in veins, workers at work, soldiers in uniform, potatoes
in stomachs, citizens in the country, uniforms in stores, IDs
in pockets, help in need, the insides inside,
hands in gloves, foreign countries outside, the tongue
behind the teeth, prisoners in prisons, meat in cans, teeth
on concrete, sputniks in space, the dead in their graves,
   the sun
in the daytime, graves in the earth, dreams in the night, the
   earth in the universe
(which is either shrinking or expanding), a gap in a CV,

9

the past in the present, the temperature in degrees,
    everybody
in his place, lifeline in a drawer, the heart
in the throat, the sky in the clouds, are there any questions

thank you, I don't see any

II, 74

This, Nothing

This, nothing,
or this: nothing's happened;
this is not yet it, nothing

to do with nothing

Only the Snows

Only snows,
only water and fire,
only the heavy earth and light air,
only the death-carrying elements,
only dead things
when they rise from the dead

or are reborn in their
next incarnations

are independent
of their works and deeds

Blow

"The blow came from the side least expected."

This could be the beginning of any account
of the origins of life on earth

or any other irrevocable event

Détente

at the same time as the trailblazing livestock
of a model farm
watched our leading artists out on a field trip
and friendly clouds
violated the airspace
of our New World,
at the same time as détente set in
across the entire surface of our planet Phantasmagoria,
painters labored for hours, did overtime
retouching the old heraldic shields,
and the skin of our old world, taut as a Buddha's cheeks,
went slack: the borders of great powers sought
their place,
peoples of the south woke up in the north
and as if in sleep, spoke in new tongues,

at the same time, when anything was possible,
a vast jammer station suppressed the signals
of nonexistent civilizations
and an ambulance siren
sliced the city into two noncontiguous parts,
at the same time, on the sill of my window
which was merely metaphorical
a drop of rain fell,
spattering every which way like an unidentified flying
    object
and I explained in vain to its surviving crew
wherein lies the distinct character of our sight,
hearing, touch, taste and smell

Cancer Wards

In wards for cancer patients
there are no cases of desertion
or defection:

on the opposite shores of humanity
wards number 13 wait

in perpetual readiness

Citizen R. K. Isn't Living

Citizen R. K. isn't living
with his wife: (or with anything
that he calls his): he isn't living by his pen,
by the indigestible Parker pen
stuck in his throat: he's a sado-
(he gnaws the wings
on his Parker pen)
-masochist (with this pen he revives the corpses
of bygone days only to subject them
to torture): born (not
knowing why): albeit to a working-class
family: he lives as a parasite (on
the tongue): an honorary
blood donor (is there no alien blood
in his veins); he's opposed to our
death penalty; crossing the border,
he tried to smuggle something: a birth
certificate, his own (collective)
organism and a pen (brand: Parker): although
he takes no notes, he communicates
telepathically: (there's a snake
in his phone and he puts one clock after another
out of commission): before falling asleep he counts to 19
84: (is he no longer counting on anything?) He lives,
though it isn't at all clear

if he deserves such a life

74/77

Like a Dream

Truly, your life is like a dream,
a train journey, a stroll down a pockmarked avenue:

it goes on unremarked, changes indefinably:

it becomes longer and longer and, running down
streets known only to itself,

it inexorably delivers you
to some lost afternoon

or generation

70

Like the Heart

Where are you rushing off to, my poor heart,

as if you were still in search
of your incarnation?

73/77

Scraps of Burnt Paper

Planets of burnt paper
are falling in the street:

only a few or a few thousand years ago
you might have thought
that heaven, too, suffers from lack of space
and every now and then it burns the files
in which it recorded every act
of everyone
who ever walked the earth;

what you feel now
you can call neither resignation
nor lack of hope

75

The Street You Cross

The street you cross
divides into two, into three:

now that you've noticed that someone
is always following you
and on the other side someone else
so that he's devoting this one moment of his only life
exclusively to following his own tracks,

be deluded no more:

before your eyes
dialectics ceases to be an empty mind game
and when it may seem to your "you"
that it's alone
it is not lonely
nor does it wander the patient earth at random:

it proves someone's need to exist

at any price

74

Sometimes, When You Say

Sometimes, when you say that it's not too late
—not now, not yet—
that nothing has yet happened
that requires your participation

your *nothing* doesn't rest
or lie in abeyance—rather, it *is*, it's
a relentless murderer;
it doubles and triples
the better to carry out its varying duties
and though its powers are inexhaustible

it sees no end to its task.

74

Who Better

Who better to understand your sense of equality
than your purebred dog?

i III 77

You Came Down On One Side

You came down on one side;
I understand, I respect your choice: we could become
mortal enemies.

But I don't think of you
as a mortal enemy
even when I'm fighting to oppose you,
defending what you, covertly or openly,
treacherously and by court order
are continually killing
in order somehow to survive
the so-manieth world crisis.

You on the other hand pretend
that you're not the one who treats me
like an enemy. (You just carry out
orders.) You, who get everything through the system,
would be happy
if I just joined the housing co-op
of mouths (tempted by the vision
of extra floor space). Maybe you think:
"—The sides are interchangeable"? There are books
no one reads? There's the proofing stage? Mitigating
circumstances? Insurance cards? The help-
line instead of the archive?

Memory that doesn't save its victims? A life
singular and unrepeatable? An extraordinary
mission to accomplish?

If you really have no other option,
be a true enemy to me. Don't break the rules
of human conflict. Don't send me your venal,
cruel and stupid hirelings. Let's be each other's contemporaries,
but don't get the idea that we are partners,
don't think that the time
in which it falls to us to live
is just a noncommittal tryout
in the theater of the future, don't pretend
that you're really not like that at all.

You aren't my adversary,
we live by different lights. It's you
who usurp the right
to speak in my name. I don't want to be
your enemy,
I don't accept your mode of combat. I could
try to understand you,
if I manage to protect myself from you,
if I manage to escape from your blind hatred.

If you want us to be
true enemies, fight me
face to face. I'm against the death penalty,
so when the fight is over
we can have a sincere and friendly

earthly conversation. Face
to face; but if one of us sees
the other is blinded by hatred or incomprehension

let us cease hostilities

1974; 76

24

By Taking Part

"By taking part in the great
Children's Health Center Lottery
you honor the memory of 2 million children
who fell in battle or were brutally murdered
in World War II.
You bring aid and relief
to thousands of children
affected by injury and illness.
You fulfill the noble and honorable
duty of a citizen.
You gain the chance of winning
many valuable prizes, such as
a Fiat model 125p or 126p,
a C-sso trailer, a television set,
radio, refrigerator, sewing machine,
washing machine

and a range of other attractive items."

High Time

This poor man
returns several times to check
whether he has really locked the house door:

high time
for the windows and doors, taps, faucets, and gas burners
to start providing attestations

even full-page loyalty declarations

X, 76

Now, When

I, the anonymous victim of a crime
don't know to this day
if I should have defended myself
or at least attempted a futile escape;

maybe not at first, when, having no other option
I went ahead and opened the door,
though I knew very well who was standing there,
maybe not yet
when I allowed them to lead me without a fight
to a discreetly parked black limo
and pretended not to recognize friends
instead of calling for help at the top of my voice,
maybe not when they tortured
every kind of confession out of me,
maybe not even when they led me off to slaughter;

at none of those moments
when I couldn't fail to realize
that human evil,
capable of everything,
prepared for anything,
is infinite
and more inhuman
then we can possibly imagine,
although evil itself is subject to every human instinct:
cruelty, cowardice, brute violence,
hypocrisy, empty talk and flattery;

maybe I shouldn't have tried to put up a defense
even when

together with thousands like myself
I dug a mass grave every day,
maybe not when my naked corpse
with a bullet through the back of its skull
and a tin tag tied to its foot,
deceptively similar to thousands of other corpses,
fell among them,
deprived like them of a face and a name;

but at the moment
when I awoke among other
living corpses
at least maybe then
I should have made a desperate attempt to escape;

which is why I'm now,
my living corpse
long since turned to dust,
still not sure
if the time has come
when I should begin to defend myself,
when I should begin to speak,
not to seek revenge or recompense

but to give testimony
to myself as well

My Poor Son

My poor son, forgive your mother,
my poor son, forgive me for giving birth to you,

I won't do it anymore.

Passing By

Passing by a house in the outskirts
I glimpse through an open window
an old man, eating alone
at a brightly lit table.

Who gave me the right
to wonder
whether he who now breaks and eats bread

may ever have been forced to betray
friends or himself
in order to survive,
whether he may not have another man's blood on his hands,

whether his face
may not have been spat on?

You Will Be Forgiven

You will be forgiven all the wrongs you committed
if you committed them
to save someone's life.

I myself am the one
for whose sake I was blind to the suffering of others
and deaf to their cries for help.

But did you really survive?

Well, I'm talking to you, I'm alive.

So that's what you call survival,
you miserable son of death?

It Was Beginning

And it was beginning to look like all of Poland
would keep its lips shut tight

and become an impenetrable empire once again

On the Eve

On the day before May Day
returning from work along grim Red Army Street
I was passing a butcher shop window
when I saw from the corner of my eye
a light-haired hand
a gold ring on its ring finger
and nails painted red
suddenly move among the cowering chunks
of real and ersatz meat.

Nothing happened.

When Price Hikes Were Ratified

When price hikes were ratified
the deputies were first to resort
to the full arsenal of socialism.

The army. Hospitals. Prisons.
Volunteer reserve forces
and special militia units.

The grass worked relentlessly.

July 2, 1976

for Leszek Sobocki

Combatants in brand-new uniforms
listen to speeches,
their tin medals clinking.

Greenery. Life like butter
melting in the heat,
the nylon flags can barely breathe;
the country, a bulging drop of ink,
hangs on a golden pen
suspended above a sheet of paper.
The cuckoo coos,
a sundial silently sounds
someone's final hour.
In the palm house peyotl grows carefree
and infantile axolotl larvae multiply

without bearing any closer
family relation to us

Lighter and Cheaper

This is not a country
that exists only on maps,
it's only here
you can really make a living:

life here is forever
getting lighter and cheaper
lighter and cheaper
than air,

air
doesn't hinder your movements,
doesn't raise itself above you,
doesn't kill,
doesn't lie and betrays
nothing
of what it sees and hears,

you new arrival from another world,
we both breathe the same air

but I breathe it differently

You'll Never Be Cured of Hatred

Pitiful newspaper, you'll never be cured of hatred;
wouldn't you do better as a dog,
which may be servile
but is still able to minister to its own wounds,
or better still, a fox, even with the wounds it suffered
in its escape from a trap;

but you, even if you are a fox or a dog,
prefer to sink into a deep sleep, a coma, progressive paralysis,
turn rabid, foaming at the mouth,
infecting other animals and humans,
finishing off your victims,
fawning over hit men,

and burying deep
the never-healing wound of truth
licked in solitude

like the most shameful affliction

Maybe I Only

Maybe I only dreamt
of a great building in K.'s city center
made of cement, without windows or doors,
with a slogan emblazoned on the facade:

THIS IS OUR START TO A BETTER FUTURE

but I woke up
as the E at the end of the sign
and self-servingly blessed fate

that I wasn't at the start.

O

Optimism grows from day to day:

from day to day its *O* inflates
in contrast to its *O*, its *p*
(which is where pessimism starts)
neither grows larger or smaller in size
and remains itself
(objectively in the same place,
subjectively shrinking in size).

O, other words seem to fail you:

you speak through the *O*,
you spy through the *O*,
you listen in through the *O*,
you satisfy the intimate needs of the *O*,
falling asleep with a fat *O* in your mouth
you awake with an even fatter one:
you are more and more open,
your mouth opens wider and wider,
not to scream, not to laugh,
not apropos, beyond belief;

it's beyond belief: you awake with a letter,
a number? a vowel? in your mouth,
with a burgeoning *O*,

which sees no world beyond itself

Infinite Number

An infinite number of straight lines cross in your heart;
these lines have neither beginning nor end

So It's Still Possible

So it's still possible that in broad daylight
under the indifferent eye of the sun and museum experts
on our city's old market, near the pillory,
the museum of the worker's movement, the arts council
office,
the museum of armaments and other temples of secular
rites
among the folk music groups, optimists of every
stripe, the dust, the servants of culture and prosperity
and other mementos of the future
(which more and more often gathers unseen
at our backs),
some peddler? caretaker? warehouseman?
lays out a display of brand-new *P* patches and Stars of David
"Authentic, straight from Auschwitz and the Łódź Ghetto!"
(so he praises his wares),
praises his wares
to beat out the competition, which not far away
is doing a lively trade in chips of soap
("Authentic soap from Mauthausen!"), believe me,
when it came to asking the price, courage failed me
and I didn't know what I should do,
and I still don't know,
but I can't stop thinking about it, although since that time

life hasn't spared us new troubles and worries

VI, 76

What Luck

What luck: two survivors from Nineveh,
Pompeii, from the ghetto of Drohobycz,
we meet at the Central Station
erected on the ash, breath and dust of the dead,
the murdered, the nameless, those who perished without a
    trace,
and we remember our dead,
murdered, nameless affairs, those that perished without a
    trace,
the immortal sky and dead landscapes,
liberty, equality, fraternity, compassion, altruism,
    understanding,
alpha and omega of smoke shallowly buried in the
    displaced air,
shreds of burnt paper, ghosts of letters and books,
carried further and further, higher and higher on streams
    of air,
crossing all inhuman, moveable and death-carrying borders,
specters of burnt books, disintegrating at a touch,
specters of our old and new, dead and living persecutors,
and we remember our old teachers
and girls now living only in our hearts

and the unceasing clicking of their shoes
behind ghostly windows

But Above All

I pray to You
with my poor words,
an end to hunger, injury,
incurable disease and suffering;

but above all
O Omnipotent Origin,
Who burdened us with freedom,
leaving us to resolve
all our human and inhuman affairs,

O Omniscient one,
Whose Name
I so rarely dare use;

strike me down
rather than ever let me
kill anyone
in the name of any faith,

strike me dumb
if I ever
in the name of any truth

seek to raise myself above another

Too Early

for Jan Lebenstein

Our fears come too early: of incurable diseases,
earthquakes, wishes suddenly fulfilled, unexpected journeys,
delayed telegrams and someone's gaze fixed on the back of
    our necks

whereas it will all come in its own good time,
without any particular hurry—but also without delay,
exactly when its hour strikes,

not necessarily at first in its final shape,

gently and soundlessly, leaving no trace in the sandy
    landscape
like the scheduled departure of a train
or a movie showtime

I, 76

Issa

for Danuta and Adam Zagajewski

Issa, of whom we know little more
than that he suffered poverty and deprivation all his life
and that happily he lived to old age,
says in one of his untranslatable poems:
"Climb Mount Fuji little snail,
but slowly, slowly."

Do not hurry, word and heart.

(The heart comes second)

I Don't Know

I don't know if a poet
can be as impartial
as a doctor, giving equal care
to sworn enemies

since a poet has to take sides
as only a sister of mercy can,
most patiently ministering

to another's suffering

VII, 77

Who Else

When I think
that I may never
right the wrongs I inflicted involuntarily
with my uninhibited words,

when I think of it,
immaculate snowflake of jasmine,
who else is there to whisper

with our lips

There Are Words

There are words which, growing rampant in our mouths,
do nothing but suck our blood

Before You Even Think

Before you even think, spit it out,
spit that word out now—
a bee that, overeager, found its way
into a mouth

capable of anything

X, 77

Clouds

Clouds sail above us—visibly and covertly,
and feel surprise at nothing and at nobody

28 VI 73

You Can Save Yourself

Save yourself by speaking the truth
—and nothing but the truth—
the double agent will say to
somebody's doppelgänger
who stumbles into a situation
in which neither cowardly heroism
nor bold fearfulness
will help in any way;

at most a sudden call of nature
or a glass of tea
knocked over by a clumsy gesture
will defer for a moment

the final solution

74

You Know Best

How can I not be afraid of you, pride's hireling;
aren't you yourself afraid that you're a victim
of your own fearful violence
and lack of imagination along with too much power?

You know best
what you're doing—like someone
who breaks into a house
under the pretext of calling for help
or offering it
only in order to strip it
of every remainder of hope, trust and faith.

Fearing so for yourself—don't you fear yourself,
slave of nothingness,
you who try us sorely,
you who lie in wait for our slightest movement,
the merest doubt, shade of disbelief
in the meaning of our world

and though you use all the products
of human ingenuity

—set back humanity by centuries

76/77

It Figures

It figures
that the torturer and hitman
regardless of progress made
in their inhuman professions,
at times have to work like slaves
to perform their varied duties well

but this is no reason to expect
our understanding for their work, our admiration, sympathy

let alone a sense of shared responsibility

No Need

No need to look for them,
they will be found, slaves
inclined to wield a power
that only love

and a fatal disease
can have over us.

This Moment

This moment has already ceased to exist

although it's neither greed, nor empire, nor faint-hearted
tyranny

Much Simpler

Your heart broadcasts and receives the signals
of civilizations dead and not yet born

the brain is a city wiped out in a distant future
grave robbers erect new mausoleums

fingerprints circulate in unfathomable space
card indexes faded, were burnt or shredded

your *you* is astonished at your *I*

nothing's for sure took the elevator down
while *everything's possible*
was laboring up the stairs

you'll get used to it you'll get used to it
it's all much simpler than it seemed

You Receive Letters

You receive letters with stamps
that portray some country or another as a banner
fluttering in the wind;

a letter's white corpse unfolds and folds its hands
a letter's white dove unfolds and folds its wings
and the wind that makes the flags flutter,
the wind wrapped in flags
behaves in accordance with its own nature

If You Open This Letter

If you open this letter,
which has finally reached you
after taking such a very long time,
and a bulging eye falls out,

don't be surprised, honestly,
because what am I supposed to do
if I have to be surprised every time
at the end of a phone call
an ear falls out of the receiver
dragging everything else with it
including the anvil

and little hammers

Quiet

Quiet, shush, woodborer:
the censor's writing

about freedom of speech

Wastepaper, Trash, Scrap Iron

Atlantologists of the future,

our small victories and great defeats,
our small truths and great lies,
our paper cities,
our incurable diseases,
our radioactive dust,
our fickle hearts,
our anesthetized minds,
our little hopes and big delusions

really existed.

These layers of limestone
are our bones.

These imperishable plastic objects
weren't our talismans, we had them
in daily use.

These glass-screened boxes
were not our gods, although often
they were used as a means
to subjugate our will
and break our spirit.

It was not unheard of
for even our thoughts to be listened in on.

The truth is also
that we multiplied like beasts

and fed on our brothers: animals and plants
having no other way to perpetuate
our own kind.

We should not have murdered each other
in the name of the inhuman Chimera
a better future.

Atlantologists of future time,
wastepaper, trash, scrap iron
if they endure
may not be the best testimony to us
but we existed all right

and we were conscious of our existence.

There Are

There are world wars kept under wraps
unnoticed cases of pneumonia and heart attacks

There's No Other

Birth is not for everybody?
Life is not for everybody?

Freedom is not for everybody?
There's no freedom for freedom's enemies
or deniers,
there's no freedom either for the living
or the dead,
or for those who for years
have been living in apathy?

There's no freedom
but the freedom that scares you so much,
there's no freedom

but freedom of conscience?

You Don't Have To

This same day, cut off the phone
or, having dialed the number for nothingness,
hold the receiver up to the pink screen
at the hour of the evening news;

or don't dial, after all you don't at all have to
hold life in your index finger

Every Day

Although I mean nothing to you
every day you
mean more and more to me,

my indefatigable Soviet watch

Maybe It's You

At long last I'm
on terms of equality: I'm
always short of time: I go to work
on my hind legs: maybe it's you
in the crowded tram, hating

(some me?)

How Far

I'm made up of cells:

yet how far I am
from their inhuman perfection

8 XI 76

Too

Clouds freely cross borders
and violate the air space of a neighboring country,
ocean waves overflow
the bounds of territorial waters,
the Universal Declaration of Human Rights
cannot be compared with particular constitutions,
constitutions are less practical
than penal codes:

from the moment states
that allow you to go without a passport
only to your grave
start praising the natural environment
nature's fate, too,

seems sealed

72/75

I'll Remember That

Remember
that I'm your friend:

you can tell me everything.

You can tell me everything, too.

I'll remember that,
stone.

25 VII 77

That's My Heart Knocking

I knock on my country's door,
the door of a homeland
shut tight and nailed up

my homeland doesn't want to become a mother
it prefers to remain indefinitely pregnant:

a poor man's heart
shuts out a poorer

Crowded Bus

A crowded bus, its destination *Border*,
cruises the streets—
sometimes running late,
sometimes early, ahead of schedule—
stops at a red light
and moves on,

for a moment reflecting our heads
cut off by the edge of the window

VII, 73

If It Comes

If it comes to the point that I shout
"Long live Poland!"

—in what language will I have to do it?

Nothing Yet

I have done nothing yet,
I barely know who I am,
but you've hated me for a long time now
as a traitor, a murderer, a mortal enemy;

I still haven't caught up,
I haven't grown into this kind of hatred—

but one day I may begin to defend myself:
I may begin to run away from you:
for I know there are flights that cause you more pain
than the most intimate blows

and you yourself know this best,

my love, my death

76

You Are

Whether or not
you acknowledge me
you are my only homeland;

you are my only homeland, silence,
you who hold all
futile words;

mute clouds,
clean breaths of our dead,
plants' riddling glances,
a postal dove with someone's letter
that perished without a trace;

you are my homeland, quietness,
crying out
in every language at once;

like the victim of a fire
who lost everything that would burn,
like a refugee
captured near a camp,

I
though I am no longer a child
nor your prisoner,
know that even in exile
I'll remain in you, native speech,
and you will be in me

like a swollen tongue: a heart,
that binds us to life

until

XI, 77

Our Life Grows

Our life grows like astonishment and dread
forgotten for a moment in a lover's arms,
our life grows like a line for bread;

our life grows like grass, like dust and moss
like a spider's web, hoarfrost, a colony of mold,
our life grows uncontrollably like a cough or a laugh;
in spite of wars, ceasefires, prophecies,
détentes, the Iron Curtain, the League of Nations,
the Cold War, climate change, the U.N.,
hidden profits and brazen tyranny,
pompous black limousines and soulless judges,
the blinding of people, the blindness of nature,
the race of generations and arms, rival delusions,
the turpitude of servants, subjects of nothingness,
lost objects and plastic dreams,
toxic newspapers and heart transplants,
secret deals and blatant lies,
the mockery of what we hold sacred,
air pollution and earthquakes;

our life grows inexorably, on heaps of rubble
and through the soundest sleep,
above us, around us and through us, we who are
its prodigal sons,
our life grows like rising prices, science fiction,
arrant inflation and speculation,
like high blood pressure, a mirror's reflections, fiction's
     tyranny, hope,
a fear of being late to work or meeting someone's eye;
our life grows like a fruit and like hunger,

our life grows like flora and fauna
but our life grows not like hatred, an urge to strike back,
or lust for revenge
and even when it doesn't know what it wants
our life wants to live

like a human being

Even When We Come Across the Speechless

We, washers of corpses, midwives, mothers,
like it or not, come to know the most intimate
human mysteries
and we don't lack for work
even when we come across the speechless
or prodigal sons

who disappeared without a trace

O Rose

Open mystery, simple labyrinth,

you lighthearted, immortal,
ominous rose, I don't yet wish,

I don't yet have the right to die

28 VI 74

I Can't Remember

I can't remember
what great happiness came to me
in my dream.

Just as in life, my owl-eyed moth.

My Daughter Learns to Read

My little daughter, faultless until now,
is learning to read and write
and only now does she begin to err

and I live my old errors of humanity
all over again.

I/VII, 77

Moment, You Were

Moment, you were my beloved,
I held you, fleeting, in my failing arms,
I was incarnate in you,
a living anchor,
when at a somber dawn
my pulse beat in you,
repeating syllables of the eternal source

and only a mute door
choked on its own tears

My Beloved

My beloved, just a moment ago
you were walking in your favorite black dress
in sunlight that lit up
the shadows of shifting triangles
(legible even to me, never
a great expert in geometry):

I stand in a cold sweat,
an implacable straight line
pierces my heart,
between us not even the smoke
of a train that departed years ago

but in the labyrinths of print
this intimate distance

weaves its web of stone

My Beloved in a Circular Dream

In a circular dream, my beloved
flees from quotidian ghosts.

Her weary body
refuses to obey,
refuses mutely:
my beloved
can't call for help
even in a whisper.

She is awoken only by the bite of a mosquito
which, though it sucks her blood
turns out to be an ally
in this unequal struggle.

Furies and vampires
are left on the other side
not having snatched even a black thread

from her favorite dress

Inscription on a Chinese Dish

I am like this dish: you can only accept me,
but don't try to change me
or fix me

Books, Paintings

Books, paintings, an amber necklace,
an apartment, if we live to see it,
the sky's pupil, a drop of dew,
a tiger conch, a passport, memory,
a human homeland without army or borders,
wedding rings, divorce, photographs, manuscripts,
five liters of blood (ten all together), hunger,
the owl of Minerva,
we may lose everything,
everything may be taken away from us

except independent,
nameless words,
even if they only sailed through us;
except words, which even if
they were written down in the dead tongues of ice

will be resurrected in the flesh

(Sleepless, It

is I
who, though hungry and sick,
left the house
when hunger and sickness reigned there.

I am: there is no me. Struck dumb,
long forgotten,
it wanders the deserted streets.

By night: one of many; the only one.

In someone's dark window
lashed by the cold light of the moon
a shadow flits.)

It hangs
on the cross.

(Forgive me.
And You, and You.)

XI, 77

Pass It On

Independent of nothingness, let us pass on
the sky-high writing of the clouds,

let us pass it from mouth to mouth.

Answer

After talking to a potential publisher
I myself don't know
who's the author of the book.

(The state, the paper, the phases of the moon
or some other circumstances?)

My answer will be partial:
the author of my book

is the Polish language

73/75

* * *

Truly: give me the finest Swiss watch
and it will start to stutter, hesitate, falter,
fear those who are just executing orders
and underestimate more real dangers,
for years want to answer a letter and fail to,
liberate spiders and their potential victims
that fly in the open window
and buzz carefree among books
bought with a last bit of cash
probably not for this life but the next,
turn to look at women (Krystynka, this
is just the Swiss watch talking),
cross out "I'm sorry that...," try again,
constantly feel as if its pants are too big,
regret mistakes (especially those not made),
repent and work virtually for peanuts,
come back but turn around at the door,
tremble at the damp, at a sour look, at any shock,
not live at any price

decompose after death

Almost All

it's the twentieth century,
I go to bed with a newspaper,
within reach lie
my glasses, pills and watch;
I don't know if I'll sleep,
I don't know if I'll wake

that's all

XII, 77

And We Really Didn't Know

(Early Poems)

The Tongue, That Untamed Flesh

for Zbigniew Herbert and Mr. Cogito

The tongue, that untamed flesh that grows in a wound,
in the open wound of the mouth that lives on false truth,
the tongue, that beating heart laid bare, that naked blade
that is a defenseless weapon, that truncheon that beats
 down
the defeated uprisings of words, that animal, daily tamed,
with human teeth, that inhumanity that grows in us
and outgrows us, that animal fed on a body's poisoned
 flesh,
that red flag that we swallow and spit out with the blood,
that forked thing encircling us, that true lie deluding us,

that child that, learning the truth, lies truthfully.

Not a Poem but a Confession

Forgive him who stopped amusing us
with the empty play of appearances:

was he not to be clear-sighted
in the face of our blindness,

was he to fall mute, living among mutes
and those with tongues torn out by blind hope

so that unable to speak
they choked on a laugh

Our Special Correspondent

for Bertolt Brecht's "Solution"

from a white house with red windows. From a white mine,
  from its
red windows, our special
correspondent reports from a white house with red
  signboards
in black-and-white newspapers. Our special correspondent,
  a waiter, brings dishes and
                              digests the reports
of an echo. With a voice that carries, and a voice that
  carries information: about weapons,
                              hidden in the blank verse
of a red network, the network of the universe. The
  universe of spies. Our special
                              correspondent in the network
of journalists and spies
imagined by a sick man. Imagined spies. In the network of
  binding words.
                      Deported to the Siberia
of the new
world,
our (special) correspondent reports on who—unanimously—
                      abstained from the vote for
                      reasons of poor health
and social services. Abstained from a vote of protest. Also
  who, unanimously
—or univocally—confused an echo's report with
a gunshot's, a multivocal revolution with a univocal
  resolution, the muzzle
of enlightenment with the enlightenment of the muzzle.
  In a game

of chess
played from inside. A unanimous guarantee and a guarantee
    of unanimity,
                         simultaneously
                 bringing a vote (a binding
word) to the ballot box: a box of ashes. Simultaneously?
                 Unanimously? However
you remove your hand in this public
secret vote
the press
of presses
will crush it the day after tomorrow. However you remove
    the veil. The veil
of exile. Our special correspondent reports
from the White House: although it's another church and in
    it the bells ring
                 unanimously. For delivery
of a report. Unanimously one-headed. Without crossings-out
    and without a choice.
                    From the white
house with pink signboards hidden in wallets
made of pigskin

embossed with a design

February 1968–April 1972

And We Really Didn't Know

for Adam Michnik

Maybe we were children, we'd seen nothing yet,
we only knew we were forced to believe in a lie
and we really didn't know what we wanted
apart from respect for human rights and truths,
when, gathered on a little square
around a monument to our great poet,
who spent his youth in an unfree country
                              and the rest of his life in exile,

we smoked cigarettes and burned lying newspapers
we smoked cigarettes though they poisoned our bodies,
we burned newspapers because they poisoned our minds,
we read constitutions and declarations of human rights,
and we really didn't know that the rights of man
can turn out to be at odds
with the citizen's interests,

and we really didn't know
so many armed units could be set upon an unarmed crowd,
against us, who were still children
armed only with ideas we were taught in school
and untaught in the same school,
armed with the ideas of the poet at whose monument we
    gathered,
and we really didn't know
that all those ideas could be erased
by blackmailing speeches, provocative articles,
by the merciless onslaught of a well-fed and insolent force,
by the manifold lie of lies,

and we really didn't know the adults didn't believe us
but the manifold lie, that everything could be erased,
that you could forget it all
and pretend nothing had happened,
and we really didn't know that what would follow
would be beyond our wildest imaginings,

and we really didn't know that memory is the citizen's
    enemy,
and we really didn't know that living here and now
you have to pretend you live somewhere else, in some
    other time,
and at most do battle with the dead

through an iron curtain of clouds

Flood

Bloated bodies of morning, rumpled sheets,
letters delivered, letters detained at the border
of reason, poisoned newspapers, choking soundbites from
    the podium, marked
cards, aborted fruits, results of a secret ballot
and predictions of the future, reports by officers of secret
    daydreams,
typescripts of books written for another man's drawer, copies
of new speeches, new
turns, a broken figurehead from the Battleship *Potemkin*,
surveillance tapes and the literature of labor, vodka,
    censorship
files, if only there was a censor like that in the digestive
system, the wreck of a jammer station (ideal
machinery of nothingness), signals from outer space, IDs
    burnt
to a crisp, nylon banners, land reservations for emerging
writers, young reserves (no need to
cross out), condoms for promises to resolve momentary
    tensions,
the guy who was in a hurry (so that his old girl didn't get any
older) and removed portraits, communiqués on Nikita
    Khrushchev's posthumous
state of health, all this was swimming
in the flood-tide of words,
all this washed up in our mouths and we couldn't spit it out,
all this gushed out of the media of mass convulsion,

and rose up in the throat

71/73

Where Are They Now

Where are they now, the fine defacements:

where are they now, the fine portraits,
the flat faces open on both sides, nailed
to the many walls
of the many worlds we have known. The embellished,
retouched faces that don't change with the course of
     nature
but are plastered over from day to day with new ones
fresh from the warehouses. Those faceless faces
off to the shredder,
hurriedly torn from walls, filling the warehouses
of bygone days, the faces forever struck dumb
recycled into new portraits, hurriedly hung
on the cardboard walls
of our new world, on the walls of marches mutely
chanting. The effaced faces,
windblown newspapers
filling the warehouses of days to come, garbage
containers, death containers, factories of scrap paper, the
hateful eyes
and silent mouths that show through the new
eyes and mouths, the faces turned toward that from which
     they came,
forever returning to the paper mill

and at times, when there's a shortage of meat

even to the slaughterhouse

1/71

March 31, 1971, 7:21 PM

the whole world is watching Moscow

12,100 people are watching the match at Idraetspark
    stadium
Manchester City is ahead 1–0 thanks to Young's shot
(automatic associations with songs of the night)
everything is still up for grabs
(liberty? equality? fraternity?)

not even a funeral procession
passes in the deserted streets
an agreement of word and deed
a miner recovering from a heart attack feels good
and according to the lady who knows everything
(because she sells newspapers)
has entered the annals of history
the mine refuses to surrender his mate's body
and at another hour
though at the same time
Charlie Manson
waiting for death in the gas chamber
(automatic association with)
prophesies a universal bloodbath

sometimes you can eat live squid
and quintuplets born at a propitious time
can save a country's political system
(which is easy enough to dismantle)

the whole world is watching Moscow

a Miners fan is dying of someone else's heart attack
a militant female citizen leaves
the Department of Rape
at the civil militia's local headquarters
it's payday
no alcohol is sold today but still
some lost passerby
perhaps not yet the owner of a television
(buying a TV is your patriotic duty)
is singing the VD Blues
at the same time
a poet in Warsaw has to postpone
the date of a reading
because right now

the whole world is watching Moscow

one survived
ten miners perished
in the docks
a few hundred killed were buried in secret
the Chinese are flooding
the capitalist world with drugs
the hour 19:22 is at hand

the whole world is watching Moscow

the nation
in the course of the past—
under the leadership—
once more achieved enormous—
The Workers' Tribune is hiring a proofreader
(eternal future)
everything is still up for grabs

(faith? hope? charity?)
the Miners' defense is in disarray
the whole world is at war
patriots fight patriots
the left doesn't know where the right is
a virgin can't find her shrine
the press falls silent
journalists aren't for sale
but are given a raise
newspapers are bought
it's raining in Copenhagen
high time to quit smoking

a great discussion is raging
across the nation

Posthumous Journey (III)

One beautiful morning
you, too, can up and leave the house
never to return to it

leave the house you never had

you can wake up at Central Station in Warsaw,
a city where only twenty years ago
twenty rats replaced one inhabitant
and now polyvinyl chloride is replacing steel,
one inhabitant moves into another inhabitant,
a third into a fourth (and vice versa), at the station in a city
where there are no unreplaced people, at a station
from where, if you believe the warning signs,
there's *No Exit* (nor a sign telling you so);
maybe at the gate of a factory
inside whose walls, beside the victims of the December
    tragedy,
our shared public secret—
not yet fully born
but already drawing up a draft for its own epitaph
in art therapy sessions—
is burning out;
maybe on a square reddened
by the blood of the red, the white, the gray, the unidentified
(but all of them equally defenseless)
and pedantically blotted with sand
(the sand is already gone: covered with snow,
blown by wind, scattered by rain);
maybe in front of a workers' hostel on the outskirts
facing a billboard that reads:

"The Voice of Progress"
with the first "o" left out
maybe in a theater at a new comedy
when an ape-shit actress
(just as tanks move in a certain direction
voicing the progress of friendly hatred
in the name of the peace and security of a dust-gray citizen
who at any moment may become a moving target),
struggles to free herself from the burning safety vest
of her surface skin,
her shallow sex, her profound failure
with its faint lips;
you'll wake up someplace
forgetting your name, your parents' names,
your place of birth and fatherland, faces of false friends
under your successive faces, with sand under the eyelids,
with a shriveled tongue
and a heart gone blind;
the radio may just then broadcast a report
about someone who left suddenly and didn't return,
someone deceptively similar to you,
as is evidenced by the stamps
in his official proof of personal nonexistence, his army
registration papers (which if you happen to be male,
will be a reminder of you even when
everyone else has forgotten you), his card insuring
the wasted life and unique body of someone
you wouldn't like to meet again
but from whom you can't part, you pick up
from the ground a photograph you dropped,
the photo of a strange woman
smiling at your alien child,
the tanks will rumble toward the border
of a friendly violence,

at every step posters will warn you
against *Venereal Disease on the March*,
the tanks will counterattack, better work conditions
will be created for women in the quarries
of the immediate future and poets of the most tender age
will be protected from the parataxis currently spreading in
    poetry;
maybe you will have to explain
to the doppelgängers of strangers met by accident
that you know nothing of the fate of the as-yet-unborn
past, which can't find its shape
or its place in our lives, the baby axolotl past
born alone
after the umpteenth brainwashing,
maybe you'll meet Jan Palach,
a twenty-something boy from Central Europe,
your contemporary,
who voluntarily burned in the mobile crematorium
of back-up forces sent to the map of future borders,
on the blades of bayonets, maybe you'll meet him,
an inhabitant of an equally tragic country,
from which your mobile country
received Christianity centuries ago;
maybe you'll meet the twenty-something Rafał Wojaczek
who hasn't yet come back,
maybe you'll meet Tadeusz Borowski,
Andrzej Bursa, Marek Hłasko, who outgrew their own
    hearts,
the sinful saints of your youth,
when you sought truth—instead of understanding,
when you sought truth—instead of justice,
when you sought truth—instead of hope,
when you sought truth—instead of faith,
maybe an amused Soso Dzhugashvili,

who was a child once, too,
or maybe Judas, unhappy prophet of provocateurs,
whom no one even wanted to nail to the cross,
so he hung himself on the cord of a help-line with a busy
   tone,
maybe you'll meet nobody,
Party or non-Party, believer or unbeliever,
maybe you'll meet workers from the dockyards of the
   universe
with their tongues shot through,
with stigmata on their shot foreheads,
maybe you'll meet nobody, maybe you'll meet disenchant-
   ment
which never lets you down,
maybe you'll meet nobody
when you, too, suddenly leave the orphanage, the men's
   home, the care home,

never to return

18 III 72/29 XI 77

Song

you won't be killed—or banished from your homeland
you won't be thrown in jail—or made to wait
over a decade for the vacancy left by the loss

of your youth—you won't start a family—you won't be
    crushed
between the pages of a book—or sent into forced exile
for a free cure at a closed facility—and at the same time

when you won't rot inside an imaginary illness nobody else
will live off your existence you won't be beaten
in interrogations or at any hour of the day or night

you will not have to answer stupified questions
nor will your near-and-dear have to lock the door
in your face you will not be tortured

in the broad daylight of your somber times in the eyes of a
    crowd
the flat slaughterhouse of the newspaper won't spit out
    anyone's pulverized bones
you will not be a sickly bird or a rabid rat

that doesn't want to remember anything and only flees
    itself
you won't be persecuted or replicated you won't grow old
before your time you won't be a blind shadow

beset by the agents of your own body you won't fight
with smoke rain or clouds you won't be ashamed of the
    truth
about your times a dark anti-Utopia you won't be killed

you won't be killed—nor fired from your job
nor kicked out of your homeland—nor allowed to return
to the ruins of a dark dream that neither warns nor
    threatens

the shallow grave of the newspaper won't spit out your
    pulverized bones
onto the pounded pavements you won't be thrown in a jail
darker than the one you carry inside you won't have to
    change

anything in the darkness of your best of all times won't be
    killed
you won't be nailed to the stake of false pride you won't be
    left
amid your objects you won't stand naked before the alien
    tribunal of the Earth

you won't have to change your name, state, faith or
    confession,
you won't be—won't have to be—won't be without guilt
you won't be the subject of a final interrogation or audience

because you believe that only a comet can change anything
and not even Nothing will be left of us

Farther and Farther Away

It's getting harder to believe

when you're standing on a train platform
every so often cargo trains go by
loaded with tanks or cars
carried farther and farther away by the metaphors
of someone's fear and daydreams
by soldiers in camouflage
and indeed the uniforms recall man's natural
environment for which
for whom we're still fighting

workers who've just come back or are setting out on a
    journey
drink light beer sitting on spread-out copies of the *People's
    Tribune*
their heads are getting lighter and lighter their workers'
    tribunes
are falling apart
this is how reality apes the poetry
that attacks it

delegation officials carry their brains in briefcases
small countries are increasingly becoming playing fields
for great powers
and nothing changes only disbelief and the deficit of hope
grow greater and greater
change into empires sit alongside great powers
form friendly alliances among themselves
it's true human longing changes its language but it says
    the same thing

there are still dreams that exploit the waking world
the hunters and hunted
believers in ideas and manipulators
and nothing changes

underwear still changes
nature changes
we still have the courage to change our underwear
and fight climate change

but even nature
as she accedes to power
will deprive us of power over our arms legs minds and
    hearts

Every So Often

Every so often someone has burned on the stake
—sages, madmen, chance witnesses
who could be any of us—

women, who on every bed
of their chance age
burned like books
for imagined and real commerce with imagined and real
    devils

like books bound in our inhuman skin

those voting for, against—and those abstaining from the
    vote

every so often our bad times turned to worse

and then the proprietors of nations claimed that it was
    getting better
and would get even better
the longer the speeches lasted—the longer the bread lines
    got,
those last in line felt behind them, too close, the bronze
    brow
of time at their heels

Some smoldered in concentration camps
in the gulag of the far north
of their best of all possible times,
they perished without a trace,
others knew but couldn't believe it,

or knew but didn't want to believe it,
anti-Fascists died at the hands of anti-Fascists,
hunger and crowding called forth our worst instincts,

every so often in the encyclopedias of our best of all times
epithets switched places, slogans came and went,
streets changed their names, some words disappeared from
    newspapers
and other words appeared,
behind which were hiding the annihilation of whole
    generations and peoples,
readers opened their papers and at the same time closed
    doors
leading to the real world,
the word god was given less and less space, the word
    human sounded ambiguous,
the curfew might go on for years

every so often
we killed time, spent our lives,
we spent time, killed our lives,
many rotted in the prisons of their chance age,
many times the treacherous knife of another heart pierced
    our hearts
there were outlaws
and those who tried in vain to make it across the borders
of their accidental ages

the struggle for peace consumed as many victims
as the struggle for power,
someone, instead of fighting the inner enemy
who got hold of his heart,
betrayed his friends,
every so often

the red pencil of death's dumbstruck censorship
which mostly employs graduates in History and Law
crossed out someone's face cut open by a bayonet
and lost long ago by its accidental owner and prisoner

of the hastily slammed covers of a membership card
of an impromptu union of trusted conversation partners,
a trusted union of impromptu conversation partners,
a cosy association of forced conversation partners,
a forced association of cosy conversation partners,
a private union and so forth of his age

every so often
these IDs with slammed shut faces
burned on the stake,
smashed the glaring bodies of presidium tables,
consumed the red cloth of an inhuman world
nylon flags swelled with artificial blood,

every so often our hearts and faces were like passing
    banners,

every so often we were on everybody's lips,
everybody's mouth received us or spat us out
the young fought the old, the old the young,
there was no equilibrium to be found,
for the former got old faster than the latter mustered
    courage to speak

and so we outstripped our time

what we called happiness—youth—
we received as a gift of nature, not of the states who
    owned us

some rotted in psychiatric prisons or camps,
others were awarded honors and fat pensions,
shady middlemen became ambassadors,
every so often history, whose graduates mostly
work in death's dumbstruck censorship,
showed some to be right and proved others wrong,
every so often our sated peers
deprived us of the means to live out of envy or stupidity,
every so often monuments to the laureates
of their accidental time were demolished
and victims of those laureates of a past age
were posthumously rehabilitated

every so often Stalin's embalmed mummy
was ready to come back,

every so often professional killers
established the death sentence,
the cancer of lies kept the age rolling along,
the age that like anyone mortally ill believed blithely to
    the end
that it was rolling along on its own strength to a better
    future

every so often we had no time
to try to change our times,
to distinguish our single lifetime
from the many times in which we had to live,
politicians, preachers, artists and poets
always found something to justify them,
sometimes we just wanted to survive,
because we believed that freedom was the conscious
    necessity
of living in our best of all possible worlds,

which was building an even better, more finely-tuned
    world
and could no longer find a single free space, a single lacuna

in the universal happiness

Blank Space

in memory of Bruno Jasieński

The Planet Phantasmagoria

We survived the war—we'll survive the peace:

every so often we believed that events of times past
would never repeat themselves
and it's true, they never repeated themselves
(but followed one another),
childhood vanished for good,
lost youth would not return
and no one counted the cost
of the time we squandered.

We lacked faith
and so we believed in anything,
in every false battle,
but didn't believe in a solitary battle, because each of us
who risked it
had to do battle with iron shadows,
with the iron stuff surrounding him,
stifling him, making a laughingstock out of him;
it was harder and harder to move,
the stuff of lying truths stopped up our ears,
even modest hopes became more and more difficult
to fulfill
and the faster we covered great distances,
the more time we needed to come to mutual understanding,
the farther we ran into the future
the longer became the path from heart to heart,
the more we knew of the lives of others,
the living, the dead and the unborn,
the less we recognized ourselves,

the media of mass convulsion
painlessly acquainted us with the world's current
    tragedies,
we still managed to worry
about our domestic flowering plants and animals
but we were terrified at the mere thought of small
    countries
being the testing ground for great powers,
we voted—silently,
we only manifested our presence
when our amateurs played against pros,
the stadiums then shook with the screams:
they changed into sky-high barricades
which no one attacked
because they'd long been captured.

How could we know
that there were poets living in our times
whose existence went unmentioned by the venal papers;
and so we didn't recognize and come to hate words
since even simple words began to lie.

If we were women
our hearts closed the more firmly
the more our eyes were opened;
if we were men,
our arms fell to our sides
the higher our earthly dreams soared,
the tighter the borders of our language closed around us
the more our tongues burst our mouths.

So many times we went back to basics
that we lost the ground under our feet

and didn't know if we'd earned the right
to die for our uncertain faith,
or keep it like a flame, a sip of water, a bite of bread

for the blackest hour

73

An Overworked Laborer of the Eternal Pen
Suffers for Millions of Failed Readers

Everything is allusion, every man's a murderer
of his previous and incipient incarnation,
too much blood flows in the veins of today's man and
    citizen,
verily, only pure art expresses the essence of today's world
thinks the overworked laborer of the Eternal Pen
increasingly superseded by the office phone
at a lecture about political allusion in contemporary Polish
    poetry
given by a speaker called X
to the employees of the security services and guardians of
    art's racial purity
—and diligently notes down the allusions
meticulously laid out on the table
from speaker X's worn briefcase: Freedom Square, Red
    Square, Veterans' Association of the 20th anniversary of
    People's Poland,
verily, there are too many allusions in phone books,
too much death and blood
on the streets, squares and wastelands of the city today,
there's too much blood, we mobilized the last reserves of
    sanitation workers
but even they couldn't cope with drying the pages of the
    last Bloody Sunday,
the rate of traffic accidents is rising,
so let's quickly build a pipeline connecting us to the
    nearest wasteland
and in the worst case it can serve as a pneumatic message
    system
(of course we'll think of a way to prevent smuggling)
but for now, until that happens,

our hero thinks, verily, every bygone time is a virgin—
so let us sink the overworked tip of our pen deeper
into the body of contemporary verse
because the more bloodied the tireless tip becomes
the more blood will spill on the surface
the faster death's mouth is stuffed
with the paper tigers of the evening and morning news
the larger grows the sphere of blank spaces in blank verse
the more blank verse becomes a miniature Siberia,
whose resources we use when we are short on fossil fuels,
to stuff the eternally gaping mouth
and purer poetry will become,
transparent as the body of a city sanitation worker
suffering from leukemia

a white winter night

External, Internal

External censorship: in the comedy *The Old Husband*
substitute for the word "old" the word "young"
and for the word "goldfinch" substitute "little bird"
because "goldfinch" is what the salons
of the Principality of Warsaw called
soldiers of the Polish light infantry,
in *Midsummer Night's Dream* cross out the expression
"the walls have ears,"
ban performances of *Son of Judah* adapted from the novel
Eli Makower
because it resolves the Polish-Jewish question
in a spirit of greater solidarity of Jews and Poles,
which is damaging to the Russian cause
in our country;

internal: passing over in silence;

external: in the course of its century-long activity
it has collected a vast number of files, averages, confiscated
manuscrips and printed materials. You could treat them
as an official history of literature;

internal: leaving nothing behind,

even traces of devastation

Individual Choice

Look, at every step you have a choice:
you can choose a tour of your country's sights,
choose the bank's latest savings plan,
cross out your life so far
or choose a movie to see,
you can choose hope or fear,
pills or gas

but it's only once every four years
that you don't have to choose every second,
enough that you make up your mind

to vote without crossing out

... May Slaves

...
...
...

may slaves not strive for power at any cost,
may power govern nothing but itself,
may judges be fallible rather than venal,
may prosecutors not stop at nothing,
may the police work to reveal their own crimes,
may burglars break into their own apartments,
may censors redact themselves out of existence,
may informers deliver reports on themselves,
may customs officers look up their own asses,
may guards build the prison of their dreams
and locking themselves up to a man, from inside
throw the key into the ocean

73/74

Author's Notes

DID MAX BROD, CALLED "DEAREST"
After writing (and publishing) this poem, I came across (what I thought was) a similar thought in an essay by the late Józef Wittlin in an issue of *Kultura*.

CANCER WARDS
I probably need not add that this is an allusion to the title of Aleksandr Solzhenitsyn's novel. I hope that my reference in no way diminishes the achievement of that great Russian writer.

BY TAKING PART
Posters like this existed.

NOW, WHEN
It is with great reluctance that I (nevertheless) decide to publish this—poem.

SO IT'S STILL POSSIBLE
I should add here that I (and other people) saw these brand-new *P* patches, Stars of David and soap with my own eyes.

THE TONGUE, THAT UNTAMED FLESH
In my time I dared to oppose Zbigniew Herbert, who said that the drama of language should not obscure for us the tragedy of the world. I thought I was right—I was wrong.

OUR SPECIAL CORRESPONDENT
This poem (which has also appeared under the title "The Discovery of America") has a history of its own.

FLOOD
Published without my knowledge and in a previous form, this "Flood" provoked a newspaper polemic, in which I faithfully declare I had an opportunity to have my say.

POSTHUMOUS JOURNEY III
I must confess that this "Journey," written in the course of one sleepless and homeless night (before a general election), still gives me no peace. First published in *Oficyna Poetów*, it became the pretext for my informal interrogation at the Krakow militia headquarters (by Inspector W., to give him a moment's half-existence) which likely determined my fate afterwards. Many had a hand (as in the case of other poems) in the version published (after all) in *Collective Organism*. I would like to believe that this version is final, but I can't rid myself of a sense of the artistic imperfection of the poem, of which I know that no matter how many times I correct it, it can't be fixed (but only in the way that death can be unfixable).

BLANK SPACE
This is an obvious allusion to the poem "Nothing."

EXTERNAL, INTERNAL
The quotations in this poem derive from authentic documents of Tsarist theater censorship, published a decade ago (in bibliophile editions, of course).

1978

White Dove of a Whisper

A PROFESSIONAL critic can place a poem in a literary tradi-
tion, describe its internal structure, its hidden music. And
no doubt that's the right way to read poetry. But we laymen,
amateurs, nonprofessional readers reach for poems and in-
vest them with our own questions, fears, prayers; we con-
verse with a poem the way we converse with a friend, a piece
of music, a picture in a gallery. Our notes, made later in an
uncertain hand, are no commentary on the poem. But they
are a commentary on the events of our time; they tell us of
the different ways a poem can be read, about ordinary read-
ers and their secret dialogues with a poet. That is how these
remarks on Ryszard Krynicki's poetry should be understood.

I

A lot has been written about Krynicki's polemic with "the
world of newspapers." Why did he write about the media?
Why did he mock the daily TV news in his poems? Because
the world we lived in was codified according to propaganda
images: the official news was a kind of mandatory frame-
work. Words and slogans attached themselves to reality, cov-
ered it up, determined its shape. Life was plastered over with
newspapers, hidden inside them—the language of newsprint
obscured the truth of life. Krynicki—along with Stanisław

Barańczak, Adam Zagajewski, and a few others—gnawed his way through those stacks of newspapers packed with lies. That's how I understand what he was trying to do: to strip things bare and give them their true names; to subject the language of ritual lies to the test of his own language and thereby liberate his sensibility, confronting the two languages brutally, yet with irony. Let us see what happens when the two worlds meet:

DÉTENTE

at the same time as the trailblazing livestock
of a model farm
watched our leading artists out on a field trip
and friendly clouds
violated the airspace
of our New World,
at the same time as détente set in
across the entire surface of our planet Phantasma-
    goria,
painters labored for hours, did overtime
retouching the old heraldic shields,
and the skin of our old world, taut as a Buddha's
    cheeks,
went slack: the borders of great powers sought
their place,
peoples of the south woke up in the north
and as if in sleep, spoke in new tongues,

at the same time, when anything was possible,
a vast jammer station suppressed the signals

of nonexistent civilizations
and an ambulance siren
sliced the city into two noncontiguous parts,
at the same time, on the sill of my window
which was merely metaphorical
a drop of rain fell,
spattering every which way like an unidentified
    flying object
and I explained in vain to its surviving crew
wherein lies the distinct character of our sight,
hearing, touch, taste and smell

II

Think about it: a poet has the answer to a fundamental question. We want to know "wherein lies the distinct character of our sight, / hearing, touch, taste and smell."

What qualifies someone to carry out this inquiry? After all, the times were not congenial to the endeavor. Those late 1960s were the end of my generation's belle époque, a time of artistic and political experiments, the Cultural Revolution in China and the revolutionary rhetoric of the Paris Left, the Prague Spring, and the student protest in Poland which was finally brought to an end by an anti-intellectual, anti-Semitic hate campaign. "And we really didn't know," Ryszard Krynicki wrote years later of our unsentimental education. And we really didn't yet know that cruelty, hatred, absolute lies weren't categories only to apply to prehistoric times, that is to say, the times of Hitler and Stalin. All those hateful lies reached us on the campuses of Polish universities and on the streets of Polish cities, lies armed with rubber truncheons and newspaper poison. Those truncheons worked—how very educational they were! But we started burning newspapers, chanting: "The press lies." And that's how it went on: lying newspapers armed with the arguments of police truncheons. It was then that we understood the intimate connection between violence and lies. The truncheons and newspapers destroyed the remainder of our illusions. We abandoned our delusions and the naive hopes of youth. We were left with images: the intervention in Czechoslovakia, the army shooting at people in December 1970, our friends emigrating and our friends bowing their heads. We started a new education: how to live in despair.

III

Because you had to live, after all. Which is to say to think and love, suffer and die.

> naked, I awoke suddenly in a line for bread,
> suddenly naked in church at a class on religion,
> in fourth grade in a class on the round earth,
> I awoke suddenly at an unknown station,
>
> I awoke suddenly,
> to wander?
>
> to walk

To set out on a journey. To go on. It was the only solution, because as Krynicki writes, "my house was raided like a brothel." To go where?

Dawns, daybreaks, mysterious signs,
a journey like reading a book in a foreign language
about familiar places,
awoken to a sleepless dream on the unnumbered side
    of the world
I read this journey backwards in a language I don't
    know

So, love. But love mixed with suffering, with pain, with dy-
ing. As if the boundary between waking and dreaming, life
and death had been erased, because that's the only way that
what was dead could be returned to life, and death itself
could be, if not embraced, then at least assimilated. Poetry
became Ryszard Krynicki's journey to the other side.

POSTHUMOUS JOURNEY (III)

One beautiful morning
you, too, can up and leave the house
never to return to it

leave the house you never had

you can wake up at Central Station in Warsaw,
a city where only twenty years ago
twenty rats replaced one inhabitant
and now polyvinyl chloride is replacing steel
. . . .
maybe you'll meet workers from the dockyards of
    the universe
with their tongues shot through,

with stigmata on their shot foreheads,
maybe you'll meet nobody, maybe you'll meet
     disenchantment
which never lets you down,
maybe you'll meet nobody
when you, too, suddenly leave the orphanage, the
     men's home, the care home,

never to return

This was a warning from a homeless poète maudit, but also
a prophecy. In a world that wanted to pass for perfectly or-
ganized, in a world surrounded by cordons of special forces
and barbed wire, where people were stricken with spiritual
claustrophobia, the poet opened a vast space of freedom.
Our dreams—as Zbigniew Herbert rightly wrote—held out
longest against humiliation. Dreams were a labyrinth and
the poet became something in the nature of a guide.

POSTHUMOUS JOURNEY (I)

In front of the faded mirror she combs
her bright, her endless hair
as if she were running sleeplessly through her
alien body, immolating itself in a dream,
lost
in the white blizzard of her skin, which encloses her,
binds her and frees her

the mirror, the reflection of nothingness, the light of
     extinguished

stars, gray with horror,
looks with her alien eyes
and the moment will not pass, blind and clear-sighted,
when only the mirror exists; from the centripetal
    emptiness
the carefully polished surface
of the glass
or metal
emerges, grows

and she, twice dead in the parting,
rapidly, as if she were afraid she'd miss
the last tram

combs her hair

That's how, looking at ourselves in the "mirror...gray with
horror," we had to live.

Faith moves the heavens.
Hope shields us from hell.

What remains: love
and purgatory

IV

Love and purgatory. That is what marked us. That mark,
which we wore with pride as others would wear a Legion of
Honor medal, is hard to talk about. I met Ryszard Krynicki
sometime in the early seventies, after the Big Shock the

previous years had inflicted. It was in Poznań, I remember, at Stanisław Barańczak's apartment. I had just returned to university as an external student and was learning to think in a new way about the world around us. I had behind me an expulsion from the university, a year and a half in prison, two years of work as a factory welder. We met at the apartment where the Barańczaks lived, and wandered the streets and bars talking about politics and literature. Maybe mostly about politics, though literature was more interesting.

Ryszard and Stanisław were by then the authors of famous poems. The Theater of the Eighth Day put on a show based on Barańczak's poems. *Odra* magazine published Krynicki's notorious poem "Our Special Correspondent," which was a poet's harsh reckoning with Communist reality and propaganda. These things were widely known in Poland. What made these poets different from the huge posse of their peers? Talent? Not just talent. Rebellion? Rebellion against reality is a natural and common feature of a poetic debut. Rebellion is often just a strategy to stand out in the literary world, a way to make a splash.

Krynicki, Barańczak, Zagajewski were not like that. They gradually condemned themselves to more and more severe censorship, and later on their poetry collections, mutilated by the censor, couldn't even see the light of day. The poets started signing letters protesting violations of civil liberties and repression of the democratic opposition. Then they started publishing their work underground, which was one of the main reasons the underground press took on such importance. They didn't exist in the literary market—they chose nonexistence. They refused official recognition, prizes, appearances on TV, and features in the literary reviews. These poets—perhaps without knowing it—created a new language for speaking about reality. It's thanks to them that our generation—we of '68—could understand each other in our own words. We ceased to be slaves to alien words—we attained autonomy and freedom.

Ryszard didn't talk much; he listened closely. Staszek did, too. But each word they spoke carried a great burden of the kind of reflection and intuition unique to poets. Only a poet—I think—is able to look under reality's skin, into the folds of brain tissue, into the heart. Poetry—I am convinced—is a kind of secret knowledge and a poem is an alchemist's retort and a telescope.

Krynicki was always a metaphysical poet, one in search of a god, a poet listening closely for voices from the other world. But it was he who, in the spring of 1977 at a poetry conference in Silesia, spoke of the duties of writers of his generation in language of an extraordinary—almost journalistic—simplicity; he spoke of the meaning of "experiences imposed on us by the social and political processes that influence our individual lives" and "the individual's responsibility, or the response that reality demands from us."

He asked: "What have I, what have we done to bring out the truth about myself, about us, about the time we have been fated to live?" He spoke of "conscience" and "individual responsibility," of the need to rise to the challenge of contemporary developments in society and politics. This is how he defined "the response reality demands from us": "these are problems," he said, "which no poet can ignore who is conscious of the times he lives in."

He saw an opportunity in talking straight, not only

"through historiosophical allusions and allegories." He mused that "maybe our poetry is too impatient because it wants immediate truth." And he added: "The stylistic individualism of the new poetry derives from the fact that poetic diction has been saturated with details of current reality, sometimes to the point of overloading the poem, and above all from the fact that the new poetry doesn't identify with the enslaving mechanisms of reality, neither with its 'natural' linguistic mechanisms, which we call 'newspaper language,' nor the ones that allow one to 'subtly' manipulate that reality in order to set up an image of it which corresponds to a societal need."

He was interested in the results of such approaches: "the image of reality created in this way is in some sense an expression of automatic writing in a crippled, injured language, and so the social consciousness and the individual attitudes it shapes are all the more mutilated. The younger generation of poets had to educate themselves, because its educators were compromised and couldn't be trusted, it wanted to find itself through the attempt to build a new consciousness, a new symbolic imagination, and finally—a new culture." So Krynicki considered it his obligation to oppose "infected language and captive consciousness." And there was a moral motivation as well. He carried on a polemic with the view that "only those artists will survive who manage to turn away from reality, from its concrete details, at the convenient time.... Those who are so brave that they turn away from reality at the time when human dignity is in grave danger, [and] after a while, when they turn back toward it, may see that the faces of their friends, those who looked reality in the face and in the eye, that those faces have been spat on."

The consciousness of what Krynicki was talking about more than forty years ago was very vivid among us. Our connection to politics—serious and well-considered—was not an ideological choice; it didn't come from a fascination with power or with the political game; it wasn't based on faith in the value of parliament or the market economy.

That choice had a clear ethical and esthetic provenance: it was a rejection of the custom of spitting on people, it was a refusal to participate in that procedure; it was solidarity with those who were spat on. Being spat on was worse than being beaten. The columns of the newspapers spat on people; hatred seeped from those pages. And characteristic of that time was more the fear of being spat on than fear of the truncheon; we lived in a spat-upon world. The poet wrote:

Pitiful newspaper, you'll never be cured of hatred;
wouldn't you do better as a dog,
which may be servile
but is still able to minister to its own wounds,
or better still, a fox, even with the wounds it suffered
in its escape from a trap;

but you, even if you are a fox or a dog,
prefer to sink into a deep sleep, a coma, progressive
   paralysis,
turn rabid, foaming at the mouth,
infecting other animals and humans,

finishing off your victims,
fawning over hit men,

and burying deep
the never-healing wound of truth
licked in solitude

like the most shameful affliction

We nursed the truth—arrived at with such an effort—
like a communion wafer. And we looked the vile world in
the eye. What did we notice? That "the world still exists."
And so we lived.

Passing by a house in the outskirts
I glimpse through an open window
an old man, eating alone
at a brightly lit table.

Who gave me the right
to wonder
whether he who now breaks and eats bread

may ever have been forced to betray
friends or himself
in order to survive,
whether he may not have another man's blood on his
    hands,

whether his face
may not have been spat on?

And in this way, walking the streets, observing the spat-on people, reading the shrieking papers and the innocent snow-flakes, we began to think about God. Many of us asked ourselves if we believed. In 1971 Krynicki remarked: "A variety of religious ideas, apparently defenseless, were in their time a triumphant weapon, before religion crossed the boundaries of culture and became a weapon in the hands of manipulators, before it became an institution producing its own enslaving mechanisms, mechanisms of violence, terror, and force." Barańczak says that Krynicki is a "fundamentally religious poet." Reflecting on the dialectic of pride and humility in this poetry he remarks that "it is only against a religious background that the stance of pride and the stance of humility turn out to be noncontradictory. Humility is motivated by faith: since God's presence is reflected in the things of this world and every poem is a partial invocation of that world, poetry becomes a way of invoking the name of God (and we should limit it to the most essential minimum, in order not to take God's name in vain). Pride is also motivated by faith: since God's presence in the world sanctions our solidarity with our neighbor, and the poet's solidarity is expressed through the word—so the role of poetry, to defend the defenseless, carries a particular obligation (and obliges the poet among other things to make such use of words that every poem be a handy tool for self-defense, a condensed portion of knowledge or vision, equal in power to a slogan on the wall, an appeal on a flyer, a proverb, a joke passed from mouth to mouth, a last cry before an execution)."

Krynicki answered Anna and Stanisław Barańczak: "sometimes I believe":

I BELIEVE

for Stanisław and Anna Barańczak

The truth is: at times I believe
in the existence of the other world, I believe in ghosts,
in vampires sucking your brain and blood,
perhaps in the end I fear even more than believe
(which comes to the same thing in our time: to
    fear—to believe).
At those times I try not to sit with my back to the door,
a door has a life of its own, and what's more,
I've become superstitious, I don't talk about my dreams
or hopes aloud anymore, so I don't scare them off, I
    avoid
uttering words that could come back to haunt me,
I cross them out of old poems (and for that matter
not only I), but I won't hide the fact
that I sometimes forget these measures of security,
drink vodka, love a woman, go on a trip, think
telepathic thoughts, turn my back
to the door—which has its own life
and sooner or later will open,
and sooner or later I'll feel the touch
of that icy hand, which may only give me a sign
or may without warning tighten around my heart,
the truth is: I don't believe this is the hand
of Osip Mandelstam or Georg Trakl,
or of any other poet who, independently of the human
or inhuman death he met,

    still speaks to us with his living words.

V

We were looking for living words to a prayer; that search was an integral part of our rebellion.

We feared lies, thunderbolts, madness. We repeated:

Save me, guide me, faithful journey,
from my own lies and those of our era.
Protect me, you, Angel and Guardian,
but you, White Cloud, be my guide.

Keep me from thunder, hurricane,
immaculate truth, give me light.
Don't overlook me, little dove,
when you send us a sign from the heights.

Forgive me, evening twilight,
don't pierce me, spear of nightmares.
Don't bless me with madness,

wake me, morning star.

I think it was the critic Jan Błoński who said that a Krynicki poem is like a shot in the heart. I often reflect on the power of his poetry, which is itself so fragile and built to defend what is fragile. Beyond artistic perfection, I look for the reasons in Krynicki's particular moral perspective. I read in these poems' testimony a strange and beautiful marriage of Joseph Conrad's heroic ethics with a great metaphysical perspective. A search and assimilation of moral rigor towards himself with Christian compassion toward others. A preservation of the solitary status of a poète maudit while expressing solidarity with an injured and humiliated community.

In a beautiful essay on Krynicki, Barańczak says that this poetry has traveled a road "from excess to ascesis." I would add to that: also a path from dream to awakening, from posthumous journeys to the real breaking down of prison gates, without leaving the dialectic of solitude and solidarity. The dream was excess; awakening requires ascesis. For Ryszard Krynicki—a poet who has accompanied our lives and conversations for half a century—equal importance attaches to the resolve to name external dangers and to name internal ones. The problem of inner and outer censorship is a question as to the shape of existence. On the outside: the specter of an oppressive Leviathan. The poet addresses it, saying:

How can I not be afraid of you, pride's hireling;
aren't you yourself afraid that you're a victim
of your own fearful violence
and lack of imagination along with too much power?

You know best
what you're doing—like someone
who breaks into a house
under the pretext of calling for help
or offering it
only in order to strip it
of every remainder of hope, trust and faith.

Fearing so for yourself—don't you fear yourself,
slave of nothingness,

you who try us sorely,
you who lie in wait for our slightest movement,
the merest doubt, shade of disbelief
in the meaning of our world

and though you use all the products
of human ingenuity

—set back humanity by centuries

But what is humanity? How does it perish? How does it
grow? None of "pride's hirelings" can answer this question.
This question must be answered by everyone alone, looking
into the dark corridors of their own heart:

how does it rise from a fall? a fall
on its knees? weakened by fear or bowing down
in humility? from a cut-off sentence,
leaving you to the mercy—or giving you mercy?
from certain faith? from uncertain fidelity?
how
and against whom,
and against what does rise up,
whom does it run out to, the poem? hope?

and the fear of fulfillment?

Certain faith, uncertain fidelity, pride, and the heart's hu-
mility—that is the fate of the maudit (poet? thinker? human
being?) in our time. This is not an Arcadian image of human
destiny. Rather, it is a pretty pessimistic account of the

condition of one who won't bow down or beat down, to travesty a Barańczak poem. It seems this is the only way to reach truth and clarity of vision. What else can a person do?

Czesław Miłosz asks: "What is poetry that does not save / Nations or people?" Krynicki answers:

What is poetry that saves?
Only names, shadows
of persons and things?

What more can it be, if not restless
as the beating of a mortal heart,
a voice of

conscience
stronger than fear of poverty and death
which nations and people,
which inhuman wars and pogroms
cannot kill or

thwart?

VI

The white dove of a whisper flies down to us. We whisper:

don't shout. Don't cry out. Fall asleep.
Don't say prayers in vain.
Above your city—don't weep—
above the city, darkness reigns.

Who will survive, who will be lost,
is written in the morning's grays.
Whom the Erinyes will accost
—and whom, disgrace.

Don't pray, don't swear,
don't shout in a dream: they're attacking.
Too late. This is the hour.
They're here, Cassandra.

They've entered, Cassandra, don't weep,
don't weep even for my pains.
Above the city, a glow and despair,

above us, darkness reigns.

—Adam Michnik

Translator's Notes

THIS, NOTHING; OR, OTHER POEMS FOR INTERNAL USE
Epigraphs: Simone Weil, *Gravity and Grace*.

CAUTE
The epigraph by Leszek Kołakowski is from his introduction to *Listy Spinozy* (Spinoza's Letters), Warsaw 1961.

WHEN PRICE HIKES WERE RATIFIED
In December 1970, protests took place in northern Poland, sparked by sudden price increases. As a result of the riots, which were put down by the Polish People's Army and the Citizens' Militia, at least 42 people were killed and more than 1,000 wounded. All the victims were buried overnight, with only the closest relatives present.

JULY 2, 1976
On this date, Poland's leader Edward Gierek held a rally in his hometown of Katowice in Upper Silesia carefully orchestrated to show that the local workers still supported him and the regime, despite the violent protests and strikes that had swept across Poland the previous week in response to the announcement of price increases.

SO IT'S STILL POSSIBLE
The P patch: a patch or badge was introduced on March 8, 1940, by the German occupiers, who required that Polish workers used during World War II as forced laborers in Germany (following the German invasion and occupation of Poland) display a visible symbol marking their ethnic origin.

WHAT LUCK
The later version of this poem has "Warsaw" and "the Betar move-ment" instead of "Nineveh" and "Pompeii."

WASTEPAPER, TRASH, SCRAP IRON
A later version omits "trash" from the title and the body of the poem.

THE TONGUE, THAT UNTAMED FLESH
Zbigniew Herbert's poem "To Ryszard Krynicki—A Letter" was included in the collection *Report from a Besieged City* (1983).

OUR SPECIAL CORRESPONDENT
Die Lösung (The Solution); a poem by Bertolt Brecht about the 1953 Uprising in Germany. Written in mid-1953 but first published in 1959 in the Western German newspaper *Die Welt*:

> THE SOLUTION
> After the uprising of the 17th of June
> The Secretary of the Writers' Union
> Had leaflets distributed in the Stalinallee
> Stating that the people
> Had forfeited the confidence of the government
> And could win it back only
> By redoubled efforts. Would it not be easier
> In that case for the government
> To dissolve the people
> And elect another?
> *(translated by R. Grimm)*

MARCH 31, 1971, 7:21 PM
On March 23, 1971, ten miners were killed in an accident at the Rokitnica coal mine in Zabrze, Silesia, and after seven days rescu-ers found one miner, Alojzy Piątek, alive. On this date, March 31, in Aarhus Idraetspark in Denmark (now Ceres Park) Manchester City defeated Polish soccer team Górnik Zabrze (Zabrze Miners) in the UEFA Cup, helped by a goal by striker Neil Young. At the same

time, the twenty-fourth Party Congress was getting underway in Moscow.

POSTHUMOUS JOURNEY III

The December tragedy: see note to "When price hikes were ratified." *Jan Palach* (August 11, 1948–January 19, 1969): Czech student of history and political economy in Prague who committed self-immolation in protest against the 1968 invasion of Czechoslovakia by the Warsaw Pact armies and the end of the Prague Spring. *Rafał Wojaczek* (1945–1971): Polish poet whose life was marked by abortive studies, alcoholism, depression, and ultimately, suicide. *Tadeusz Borowski* (1922–1951): Polish poet and prose writer. His wartime poetry and stories dealing with his experiences as a prisoner at Auschwitz—published in English as *This Way for the Gas, Ladies and Gentlemen*—are recognized as classics of Polish literature. *Andrzej Bursa* (1932–1957): Polish poet and writer. Many of his contemporaries attributed his early death at the age of twenty-five to suicide; the true cause was a congenital heart disease. *Marek Hłasko* (1934–1969): Polish prose writer, known for his brutal prose style and his disillusioned outsiderdom, whose life was characterized by nonconformism and alcoholism, and who died of a mixture of alcohol and sleeping pills in Wiesbaden, West Germany. *Soso Dzhugashvili:* (1878–1953): Joseph Stalin. *Soso* was a childhood nickname, from *Iosif.*

BLANK SPACE

Bruno Jasieński (1901–1938): Polish poet and leader of the Polish Futurist movement in the 1920s and '30s, executed in the USSR in the Great Purge. In Polish, *biała plama*, translated here as "blank space," refers to the *terra incognita* on a map and, by extension, to unmapped parts of history or those, like the Soviet purges, deliberately passed over in silence.

EXTERNAL, INTERNAL

Old Husband is a 1844 comedy by novelist and playwright Józef

Korzeniowski (1797–1863). *"the walls have ears"*: In *Midsummer Night's Dream*, Demetrius says: "No remedy, my Lord, when walls are so willful to hear without warning" (V, 1). In Leon Ulrich's classic Polish translation, the last phrase is translated literally as: "when walls listen in (*mury podsłuchują*) without warning." *Eli Makower*: 1875 novel by Eliza Orzeszkowa (1841–1910) describing relations between the Polish nobility and the Jews. In 1905 she was nominated for the Nobel Prize in Literature along with Leo Tolstoy and Henryk Sienkiewicz; the latter was awarded the prize.

INDIVIDUAL CHOICE
Ballots used in the elections held in Communist Poland required the voter to cross out names of the candidates being rejected, instead of marking those preferred; from 1957 onward, frightened by the signs of the development of actual rivalry between candidates, the Polish Communist Party, led by Władysław Gomułka, appealed to all voters to "vote without crossings-out," or cast an unmarked vote, which automatically went to the first candidate on the electoral list, supported by the Party.

AFTERWORD
Adam Michnik's essay has been reproduced here in an abbreviated form.

Acknowledgments

THE TRANSLATOR is grateful to the following journals, in which some of these translations first appeared: *Absinthe, Little Star, New England Review, Two Lines,* and *Words without Borders.*

Warm thanks also to Susan Barba, Anna Bikont, Clare Cavanagh, Nawojka Cieślińska-Lobkowicz, Marysia Dzieduszycka, CJ Evans, Edwin Frank, Leonard Gardner, Katarzyna Herbert, Edward Hirsch, Ann Kjellberg, Sara Kramer, Adam Michnik, Marcin Sendecki, Bożena Shallcross, Barbara Toruńczyk, and Adam Zagajewski for the most various forms of help and support, and most particular thanks to Ryszard Krynicki, Krystyna Krynicka, and Natalia Krynicka, *sine quo nulla ibi esset liber.*